930

KT-424-241

Series 561

© Ladybird Books Ltd (formerly Wills & Hepworth Ltd) 1957
All rights reserved. No part of this publication may be reproduced, stored in a retrieval system, or transmitted in any form or by any means, electronic, mechanical, photocopying, recording or otherwise, without the prior consent of the copyright owner.

THE STORY OF
NELSON

by L. DU GARDE PEACH,
M.A., Ph.D., D.Litt.

with illustrations by
JOHN KENNEY

Ladybird Books Ltd Loughborough

THE STORY OF NELSON

Two hundred years ago a little boy, called Horatio Nelson, was born in the County of Norfolk, and grew up to be the greatest fighting sailor England has ever known.

During almost the whole of his life the English were fighting against the French, who were commanded by Napoleon, the famous French General and Emperor. It was Nelson who finally defeated him at sea, just as, later, the great Duke of Wellington defeated him on land.

When Horatio Nelson first went to sea he was only twelve years old. He was lucky enough to have an uncle who was the Captain of a ship in the Royal Navy, so Horatio was treated kindly, and quickly began to learn his way about.

But he must have felt very small and lonely as he stood on the quay at Chatham, with the big ships and the busy sailors all around him.

7214 0162 7

In those days there were no steamboats, and all the ships of the Royal Navy had high masts and sails. In order to spread the sails to the wind, and to furl them when the wind was too strong, the sailors had to climb up into the ship's rigging, high above the deck.

This was very dangerous, and many sailors were killed by falling from the yards when the ships were tossing about on rough seas.

As well as being dangerous, the sailors life was a very hard one. Their food was sold to the Navy by men whose only concern was to make a profit, and it was often unfit to eat. But it was all the sailors were given, and they had either to eat it or starve.

So very few men wanted to be sailors, and to get enough to man the ships, men and boys used to be seized in the streets by the press gang. Once aboard they could not escape, and often their families did not know what had happened to them, until they returned, years later, from long and dangerous voyages.

The ships of the Royal Navy two hundred years ago were very small compared with ships to-day. But they needed a large number of men in the crew to attend to the sails. So the sailors were crowded together on the lower decks, where it was often impossible for a man to stand upright.

It was on these decks that the sailors slept in hammocks slung from the beams, and it was here that they had all their meals. Here, too, were the guns, ready to be run out through the gun ports when the ships were in action.

As well as the sailors, there were soldiers, called marines, on board. They loaded and fired the big guns, served by boys known as "powder monkeys," who carried the charges of gunpowder up from the hold, deep down in the ship.

This was the Service which Nelson knew as a small boy. When he became an officer, and commanded ships of his own, he remembered what it was like and did more than anyone else to make the life of the sailors better and safer.

Horatio soon became very good at sailing, and when he was only fifteen years old, he was made Captain's coxswain in a ship called the " Carcass."

This was a very important position for a boy so young as Horatio. It meant that whenever the Captain went out in a small sailing or rowing boat, Horatio was in command of it. The Captain would have been very surprised to know that the small boy who ordered the sailors about so confidently was to become the greatest admiral in all our history.

The " Carcass " was not bound on an ordinary voyage. She was under orders to sail to the far north, on a voyage of exploration, amid the snow and ice of the Arctic Ocean.

Young Horatio Nelson had already made one voyage to the tropical islands of the West Indies: now he was to see the frozen seas of the far North.

After sailing up into the northern seas, Horatio returned to England and at once started on another voyage in a ship called the " Seahorse."

This time he went to India, and we can imagine him ashore in the native bazaars of Bengal. Here he would see all the strange, colourful life of the East, as he bargained with the Indian merchants.

But the climate of the tropics was too much for him. After two years he became very ill, and had to be sent home.

He himself has told us how he felt on the long voyage round the Cape of Good Hope. He was very unhappy, thinking that he would never be strong enough to be a sailor.

" Then," he says, " I almost wished myself overboard. But a sudden glow of patriotism was kindled within me. Well then, I exclaimed, I will be a hero, and confiding in Providence, I will brave every danger."

To the end of his life, Nelson never forgot that moment, or that resolve.

The long voyage home did Horatio good. He passed his examination, and the very next day he was appointed to the frigate " Lowestoft " as Lieutenant Nelson. He was now nineteen years old.

In the " Lowestoft " Nelson sailed once more to the West Indies. In command of a small ship, he soon showed himself to be a good officer.

The Commander-in-Chief took him into his flagship, and two years afterwards promoted him to the rank of post-captain. He was now made captain of a ship called the " Hinchingbrook."

This was Nelson's first real command. The young Captain, not yet twenty-one, must have been very proud as he stood on his own quarter deck.

Nelson was the youngest Captain in the Navy, but he soon showed that he was one of the best. It was not long before the " Hinchingbrook " had captured four enemy ships.

Soon afterwards Nelson took part in an attack on the Spanish settlement on Lake Nicaragua in Central America. This meant that he and his men had to force their way up the River San Juan, in small boats, at the time of the tropical rains.

The terrible journey through the forest in the pouring rain was too much for Nelson's strength. Like so many of his men, he became very ill, and had to be sent back to Jamaica.

For a long time he was very ill indeed. He had been made Captain of a fine ship called the " Janus," but he was too ill to take command of it.

So once more he was back in England. He was unable to use his left arm, and was in great pain. What was worse, he was afraid he would never be able to go to sea again.

But the enemies against whom England was fighting now included America and Holland. The Navy needed every ship and every man.

Nelson was too good an officer to be left on shore. Partly disabled as he was, he was appointed to command a frigate called the " Albemarle," which had been captured from the French.

In this ship Nelson was at sea the whole winter, sailing as far north as Elsinore in Denmark. This must have been a great trial to a man not completely recovered from an illness, because ships in those days were not as comfortable as ships to-day. They were very cramped below decks, and because there was no way of keeping food fresh, it was often bad.

It was whilst returning from Denmark that Nelson's ship collided with a much larger ship in a gale, and was nearly driven on to the dangerous Goodwin Sands.

For a time Nelson remained on shore. But when England again declared war on the French Republic, he was given the command of one of the big line-of-battle ships, as they were called.

This was the " Agamemnon," known as a sixty-four. This meant that along her sides she had sixty-four cannon with which to fire at the enemy.

It was whilst in command of the " Agamemnon " that Nelson lost the sight of an eye. This was when he landed with his sailors on the island of Corsica.

This island, on which Napoleon had been born, had been sold to the French by the Italians. The English Admiral now decided to capture it, so as to have a harbour for his ships.

The French had two very strong forts on the island, Bastia and Calvi. It was whilst besieging the second of these forts, that Nelson's eye was damaged by splinters from an enemy cannon ball.

Nelson was one of the luckiest as well as one of the bravest officers the Navy has ever had.

This was shown when, on one occasion, he sailed right through an enemy fleet without being discovered.

It was after Spain had again joined France against England. Nelson had been sent into the Mediterranean to bring away some of the English soldiers on the island of Elba. They refused to leave without definite orders from the War Office. There was nothing that Nelson could do, so he sailed away to join the Fleet.

This Fleet, under a famous Admiral called Jervis, was in the Atlantic, so Nelson had to pass through the Straits of Gibraltar to join it. We can imagine his surprise when, on a misty morning, he found himself surrounded by dimly-seen ships, only to discover that they were Spanish.

Nelson sailed quietly on, and the Spaniards never knew that their greatest enemy had been within their grasp.

Two days later Nelson had joined the ships commanded by Admiral Jervis, and they decided that they would attack the Spanish ships.

This was a very famous battle, called the Battle of St. Vincent, because it was fought near Cape St. Vincent in Portugal.

In this battle Nelson sailed his ship right up against two of the biggest of the Spanish ships. As soon as they were touching, Nelson sprang on board the first of them, followed by his sailors.

The fighting was fierce, but Nelson was utterly careless of danger, and soon this ship was captured. Immediately Nelson and his men boarded the second ship.

Many of the English sailors were now wounded, but when Nelson sprang on board the second Spanish ship, sword in hand, every man of the crew followed him. Before such a fierce attack the Spanish could do nothing, and soon this ship, too, was captured.

Nelson had come through the attack on the two Spanish ships unwounded. Now he stood on the quarter deck of the larger of them, called the " San Josef," while the prisoners were gathered on the deck below.

In those days, when ships were captured by the men from one ship jumping on to the deck of the other, it was very different from to-day. When a ship surrendered, the Captain and Officers of the captured ship drew their swords and handed them to the victorious Captain.

Nelson's bravery in this battle made him the hero of England, and a famous picture was painted of him, as he received the swords of the Officers of the " San Josef."

There were so many of them that he handed them to his boatswain, who tucked them under his arm.

Nelson was now made an Admiral. He was only thirty-eight years old, and was the youngest admiral in the Navy. He was also knighted and became Sir Horatio Nelson.

The new Admiral was in command of a number of ships. He was ordered to cruise off Cadiz, and stop the Spanish ships from sailing out of the harbour.

But Nelson was a fighting sailor, and he soon got tired of just sailing up and down. So he used to put parties of his sailors into small boats and row into the Spanish harbour on dark nights.

These raids were so successful that Nelson was ordered to attack the Spanish island of Teneriffe in the same way. But just as the sailors were landing on Santa Cruz, with Nelson himself leading them, he was hit in the arm by a shot from a cannon. This is why, in pictures of Lord Nelson, he always has an empty sleeve pinned across his chest.

Nelson wrote to Admiral St. Vincent: " A left-handed Admiral will never again be considered as useful, therefore the sooner I get to a very humble cottage the better."

But Nelson was wrong. When he got back to England he was sent for by King George III. The King thanked him for all his brave deeds, and invested him with the Order of the Bath, which is a very high honour.

Nelson found that he was now a national hero, and people cheered him wherever he went.

He found the humble cottage, but he never lived in it. Although he could not now lead his sailors in attacking enemy ships, he was the best Admiral the Navy had. Very soon he was again at sea, this time in the Mediterranean.

He was now in command of about twenty ships.

The French General, Napoleon Bonaparte, had taken an army to Egypt and conquered it. But this army could not get back to France without ships. What Nelson wanted to do, was to sink the ships.

One day he found them. They were at anchor off the coast of Egypt, at a place called Aboukir Bay.

The French ships were close to the shore, and they thought Nelson would attack them from the sea. So they had all their cannon on that side, ready for him.

Nelson had expected this. So he sailed between them and the shore, and before they could move the heavy cannon, he had sunk or captured most of them.

The fight went on until it was dark. Then the gunpowder on board the French ship " Orient " caught fire, and the ship blew up in a great explosion. When they saw this, all the other French ships surrendered.

Nelson's victory over the French fleet meant that General Bonaparte could not bring his army from Egypt and conquer Italy. When Nelson arrived at Naples with his ships, he was welcomed by the King and all the Italian people.

We can well imagine the scene in the lovely Bay of Naples. The King and his Court came out in the royal yacht to greet Nelson, and as he took his hand, the King called him " my deliverer and preserver."

Behind the town was the great volcano of Vesuvius. This, with its clouds of smoke, and the blue water of the Mediterranean, made a picture which Nelson never forgot.

Besides all this, Nelson received the thanks of Parliament and a pension of £2000 a year, as well as rich presents from people like the Czar of Russia and the Sultan of Turkey.

It was not very long before a fleet had to be sent to another part of the world. This was the northern sea called the Baltic.

The countries round this sea were trying to get all their ships together, in a way hostile to England. So Admirals Hyde Parker and Nelson were sent to prevent them.

This resulted in the Battle of Copenhagen, one of Nelson's most famous sea fights.

The Danish ships were anchored very much as the French ships had been at the Battle of Aboukir Bay. But this time the water was not deep enough for Nelson to sail between them and the shore.

It was a very fierce battle and in the middle of it, Admiral Hyde Parker signalled to Nelson to withdraw. But Nelson put his blind eye to the telescope so that he could not see the signal, and soon the Battle of Copenhagen was won.

After the Battle of Copenhagen Nelson returned to England. He was now the most famous man in the country.

He became Lord Nelson, and many other honours were conferred upon him. As England was now at peace, he was able to live at his country home, instead of being always at sea.

During this time Nelson made many journeys to different parts of England. Of course, all these had to be made in carriages drawn by horses, because railway trains had not yet been invented. So instead of rushing through little wayside stations without stopping, Nelson drove slowly through hundreds of little villages in his open carriage.

Every village was decorated with flags, and everywhere men, women, and children came to cheer their hero.

For two years Nelson lived a peaceful life on shore. Then war broke out again between England and France.

Admiral Lord Nelson was at once appointed to command the Fleet in the Mediterranean. Two days later he set out at dawn, from his home in Merton, to drive down to Portsmouth.

The same evening he went aboard his flagship. It was called the " Victory," and is the most famous ship that the Royal Navy has ever had. It can still be seen, exactly as it was a hundred and fifty years ago.

Nelson sailed at once to watch the French port of Toulon. His orders were " to take, sink, burn or otherwise destroy " all French ships.

For two whole years Nelson remained at sea. During this time Spain had joined with France, but their ships all stayed in harbour, where Nelson could not get at them.

Then a new Admiral was appointed to command the French fleet. His name was Villeneuve, and he received orders from Napoleon to sail to the West Indies, in order to draw Nelson and his ships out of the way whilst the French soldiers invaded England.

Nelson followed the French ships all the way across the Atlantic, without ever catching sight of them. Then after many days, he heard that the French Admiral had set sail again for Europe.

Immediately Nelson started back on the long voyage home, only four days sail behind the French fleet. And during every hour of daylight, sailors were posted high up in the rigging, looking for the first sign of the enemy. At last they sighted ships on the horizon.

Nelson had caught the French at last.

It was on a misty morning of October, in the year 1805, that Nelson first had sight of the French ships from the quarter deck of the " Victory."

The French Admiral Villeneuve had thirty-three ships; Nelson had twenty-seven. But although the enemy had six more ships than he had, Nelson decided to attack them.

As soon as it was light he ordered his ships to steer towards the French. When they saw this, the enemy ships turned away, and soon Nelson's sailors were hoisting every sail they could, so as to catch them.

When at last they drew close, the French were in one long line. Nelson ordered his ships to sail straight at the line of French ships, and to break through it in two places.

It was then that he hoisted the signal flags which read: " England expects that every man will do his duty." This is probably the most famous signal ever made.

As the " Victory " drew close, the French fleet began to shoot at her with all their guns. Fifty of Nelson's men had been killed or wounded before he gave the order to fire back.

Nelson was waiting until he was close enough to do the most damage. It was not until afternoon that the guns of the " Victory " opened fire.

In those days a ship's guns fired round cannon balls, or hundreds of smaller shot. Nelson's guns were double loaded with both, and soon he was able to fire them right into the cabin windows of the French ship " Bucentaure."

The ships were now so close together that the muzzles of the " Victory's " guns were touching the side of the French ship, and the men on the lower decks who were firing them, were blinded with the smoke and deafened by the noise.

It was now that Nelson's flag-ship, the "Victory," crashed into the French ship "Redoutable." Soon the spars and the rigging of the two ships became so closely entangled that they were locked together.

The French captain was afraid that the English sailors might get into his ship by way of the lower gun ports. So he ordered these to be closed, which meant that the great guns of the French ship could no longer be used.

Nelson noticed that the French cannon were no longer firing, and he thought that the French captain had surrendered. He gave orders that the English were to cease fire, but when the Frenchmen continued to shoot with their muskets, the English returned to the attack.

Twice this happened before at last the French were beaten. But by that time the English fleet had suffered a terrible blow.

In those days the great fighting ships had platforms, called tops, built high up on the masts. These were occupied by men with muskets.

From each ship these men were shooting down on to the deck of the other ship. As they were so close to one another it was almost impossible to miss, and Nelson, in his admiral's uniform, with all his medals and stars of honour, was easily recognised by the French marksmen.

Soon he was badly wounded and was carried down into the dark cockpit of the " Victory." As he lay there, with the noise of the battle all about him, he thought only of how the fight was going. He was still able to give orders, and soon he knew that eighteen of the enemy ships had been captured, and the rest were in flight. The Battle of Trafalgar was won.

The last words of this great Englishman were " Thank God I have done my duty."

Series 561